WHEN I WAS A GIRL ON BAR

by

BERTHA MILTON

I think of the days when I was young
And life was good and full of fun.
I'd laugh and I'd skip and play with the boys,
'Cause I was never much for toys.
I played in the street until it was dark
And I'm telling you straight I had many a lark.

When I got older I changed a bit.
I liked to dress up and I thought I was "it".
I wore great big hats and bracelets and pearls,
I put up my hair, I got tired of curls.
I still liked the boys though
And I think they liked me,
Because of the things they'd say, you see.

Well, when I became widowed that wasn't much fun,
I had a small daughter and also a son,
So I went out to work, with very poor pay
And my life became hard, I'm sorry to say.

Now I've got old, past eighty-three
And I think of it all, how it used to be.
I still like to laugh, but of course I don't skip,
For I know if I did, I'd certainly slip.
Yet life is still good, I'm thankful to say
And I hope, please God, it stays that way.

* * * * * * * * * * * *

INTRODUCTION

This booklet has got nothing to do with the official history of Bristol. It won't even mention Merchant Venturers, City Fathers or Lord Mayors.

It's about the lives of working men and women, in particular those who lived and worked on Barton Hill. Each week for ten weeks, fifteen to twenty people came along to a W.E.A. class at the Barton Hill University Settlement. They didn't come along to be lectured at but to recall what they regarded as important from their own memories. The meetings were tape recorded and this booklet is an edited version of what was said, of the written recollections that were handed in, and of interviews with people from the area.

Just as now working people are often seen merely as those at the receiving end of official decisions, so too their past is frequently ignored, submerged or misrepresented in official history. "Bristol as We remember it" is an attempt to redress the balance.

Ian Bild
Colin Thomas.

Barton Hill is an area near the centre of Bristol. Since the first reference to the Barton Regis Hundred in the Domesday Book, the area changed very little – right up until the 1830s it was still sparsely populated and dominated by fields and narrow country lanes.

Then in 1838 a cotton factory was built in Barton Hill. There was a great influx of people, coming to live in the hurriedly constructed houses and to work a 12-hour day in the factory.

Gradually other industries grew up in or near Barton Hill – Lysaghts, the Board Mills, and the railway. Children were born and brought up alongside the places where their fathers and mothers worked.

CHILDHOOD DAYS

Bertha Milton : Barton Hill was the place where I lived with mother, father and seven of us children. We lived first in No. 41 and then later in No. 55 Hayward Road.

Bill Nicholas : The posh part of Barton Hill!

Bertha Milton : My mother was a church woman, and rather strict, but we never went untidy and always had enough to eat and never went without our shoes and stockings. If we had bread and butter we didn't have jam or cheese. If we didn't eat at meal times all that was put on our plate we had to eat it at the next time. We shared an egg, half each and on Sundays we had afters-special. We couldn't afford real butter – only marg.

Bill Nicholas : And we couldn't afford marg. – only dripping.

Bertha Milton : My father was killed through an accident. That happened in Silver Street. I was about four years old then, so mother went to the corner shop and did housework mornings.

Hilda Edwards : I was what they called a War Orphan, so my mother had still to keep me out of the War Pension of 21/- per week until I started work.

Bertha Milton : Mother grew everything and kept fowl and soon the boys kept pigeons. So from time to time we had fowl for Xmas and sometimes pigeon pie. Mother could cook anything.

Mother always had the big iron saucepan on the hob (we had no gas stove) and with a three *lb.* ham bone, she'd make a marvellous pea soup. After baking all the bits of pieces of the bone, she'd put it in a clean tea cloth and pummel it with the rolling pin, put it in the pot with split peas and soak it all night, then add a bit of all sorts – carrot, swede, turnip and onion. It would be slowly cooking on the hob all day and when it was cold you could almost cut it; it was a jelly and it was lovely.

Life was hard for everyone, but all the neighbours were friends and very few front doors were kept shut.

Neighbours would borrow a cup of sugar, a little drop of vinegar, a bit of tea, a cup of milk, and if they had any Aunts or Uncles coming on a Sunday a lend of a white tablecloth. One neighbour had a mangle, so everyone used it after wash days; it cost 1½d a dozen. I always had that job.

Although there was the corner shop (it's closed now, but still there) almost everything could be bought in the street. Every day someone would bring a cart and call out. The Welsh cockle woman, her tub on top of her head; the milkman with his yoke on his shoulders, the baker's open cart; the fish man; eight a shilling mackerel, and the vegetable man who also sold pinky fruit. Eggs were often a shilling a dozen, which meant one extra. Sugar, tea, flour, sultanas, currants and rice were all sold at the shop and was weighed and packed from a sack that was in the shop. Nearly all people 'trusted' from week to week and if you happen to go to buy you wouldn't get served if you hadn't brought the book, which was different to buying in the street.

Ralph Bewley : Every Saturday morning, my younger brother and myself, it was our job to get all the cutlery out and clean it; then after we'd done that, we had to go across Barrow Road bridge and get a hundredweight of coal in one of they little barrows from Buffets. And he had a woman there. Well, she was old when I knew her. She had an old Victorian dress, she had what you call a white apron on, tied round the middle, an old cardigan, and a man's cap, and she did work like a Trojan. She got a hundredweight of coal and throw it in your bag. And you couldn't diddle her.

Hilda Edwards : We used to have the hurdy gurdy man round. Sometimes he'd have the monkey on top of the hurdy-gurdy and he'd be dressed as Charlie Chaplin sometimes and he'd have all us kids singing.

Rowlie Edwards : He went blind eventually. He married a schoolteacher. He used to come round with a barrel organ and as soon as we did see him all the kiddies used to sit on the edge of the pavement. And he'd have us all singing. Instead of stopping there for about five minutes he stopped there for about an hour. Then he used to go round all the houses and get a lot of money for entertaining the children.

Bertha Milton : There was a poor old woman who used to come around on Sunday mornings. She used to sing 'Where is my wandering boy tonight'. She always had a little shawl on.

Rowlie Edwards : One used to come round and sing 'Abide with Me'. Then there was a cockle woman who used to come round with cockles on her head.

Hilda Edwards : I remember on a Sunday morning a man used to come round singing while we were waiting to go to church. And my mother said, "He's taking a long time to sing this morning, you better go on or else you'll have a late mark. You won't have your text." And this Sunday morning I came up round the corner and then I looked back to see about the man singing – I was so worried. And I looked back and that man was running like the deuce. He'd had so much money in Holm Street, and he was running somewhere else to get some more money. He was a wicked man.

Rowlie Edwards : The elver man used to come round with a bath full of elvers on a Sunday morning. He picked them up with his hand and put them in your basin. – Two penny worth of elvers.

Bertha Milton : They were lovely when they were hot.

The lamp lighter came every night with a long pole over his shoulder, to put the light on and every morning very early to put it out.

All the children in Hayward Road played in the road, skipping; hop scotch; whip and top; bat and ball; cricket and often breaking a window then clubbing together to pay for the repair. We girls loved to put a rope round the lamp-post and have a good swing.

Hilda Edwards : We used to stand around by the light. At one house he said, 'I shall throw some water on you girls one night. and it shan't be real water either.' And then it was time for us to go in and I told my mother. She said 'Where have you been?' and I said only under the window of Mr. Howe. She said, 'It's a wonder he doesn't get fed up with you, making that noise, talking and laughing.' And I told her what he told us. Well, anyway we went round a couple of nights after and I missed him in the shop. I said, 'I don't know, I don't know where Mr. Howe is. I wonder if he has gone upstairs to pour cold water over us.' Well I suppose for a little bit of fun he got the chamber pot and put a spot of water in it and threw it out of the window. My mother was disgusted.

Bertha Milton : The boys in Hayward Road went round singing once, at Xmas. And the man was up in the bedroom and he told them to go away and they didn't go away, so he shouted out from the window, 'Well, here it is, part this between you.'

Rowlie Edwards : We used to go round and we always used to have a big ball of paper, tied with string, and that could hurt when you started swinging that round. We used to get outside the church on the vestry steps. About 8 of us, or 9 of a night, and say 'Right, we're going to gang up over, say, Russell Town.' And over we'd go to Russell Town. And of course they would be prepared and as soon as we got there we started swinging these strings round, till the police came along. And of course we all disappeared.

Bill Nicholas : They also used to have small cans, with rags inside which they set fire to. And twirl them round and round. Fire tins.

Bertha Milton : I'll tell you another thing they did with old tins and an old bucket; they used to kick them about, and the mothers used to say stop it, because it was a sign of bad luck.

Ralph Bewley : I met one of my old pals on Monday. I hadn't seen him for years. One of the first things he said to me, he said,

'Remember, Ralph, when it was cold, and we had a heavy fall of snow. We were about 8 or 9. We were playing on the park and this certain woman had phoned up the police several times to stop us playing.' So what the mob had done – they came out of Barton Hill school and they started a snowball and we brought him all up Jarvis Street and he went right down over Barrow Road. And by the time we got down to Ashley Street we couldn't shove it.

Rowlie Edwards : Outside of our church there were some railings and there was a crypt and we could get down there. What we used to do – one did get down the crypt, hand a piece of cotton up, put it over the lamp-post along the copings for about four houses, tie up the cotton to a door knocker, and the one who was down the cellar did pull the knocker. Of course, they did come to the door, couldn't see anyone, as soon as they shut the door, bang bang on the knocker again. One night somebody came out and noticed the cotton on the knocker. They traced it to where the cotton was. They traced it right over down into the cellar. But it was so far down, they couldn't see anyone down there. We used to play that night after night.

Hilda Edwards : I can remember when the troop trains came in and we used to run home and say; 'Mummy, the troop trains are in.' And they used to say: 'Here we are, here's a cup of tea.' But there wasn't really half a cup of tea left in the cup by the time we'd got down there. And a sandwich. Some were just going off and they couldn't even reach it. My father was killed in the first world war. Some of the soldiers were nearly crying when the train drew out.

Reg Harding : Errands to my Uncle George Withy led me to Barton Hill Baths to swim all day, and if I squandered the coffers Uncle gave me, to swim in the Feeder Road canal instead.

Rowlie Edwards : In the Feeder canal there used to be a lot of swimming. I can remember as a boy, how I used to go down there swimming, and immediately we did see a policeman, we did dive away with no clothes on; all the way up over the Brillows. And always leave our clothes on the bank. That's true. It was on a Sunday afternoon after Sunday school.

One policeman did come down the river one way and the other did come down Marsh Lane. And they'dmeet in the centre of the bridge. One couldn't cross over and one couldn't go the other way. They had to meet in the centre of the bridge. That was the end of their beat.

Ralph Bewley : And you know the bridge down here, Ducie Road Bridge, years ago there used to be a lamp in the middle and the kiddies used to swing that lamp and just poke their faces at the policeman. He daren't come over because it was off his beat.

Bertha Milton : On wet days we'd have to play in the stairs, mothers and fathers usually. I loved the boys, I really did. I didn't like the girls. I was called old Bertha-Milton-play-with-the-boys. That was a

'Mad' Harry Hyde, an engine driver, was one of those who went off from Barton Hill to the war. He kept the card his children enclosed in his wife's letter to him until he died– from the effects of poisoned gas four years after the war ended.

good thing. I had many a slap for playing with them. They'd run after me in the passage and mother would run out of the kitchen and drive them out.

All we ever knew about sex was learned in the streets, never from our mother. Some of the girls that were older told us things that used to frighten us all to death and other things that made us scream with laughter.

SCHOOL DAYS

Rowlie Edwards : I always remember the girls going to school. I used to admire them. I wasn't very old. They'd all wear white pinafores. They were starched stiff and they stood out.

Bertha Milton : And white drawers. You could step in and out of the pinafores.

Rowlie Edwards : The first school to be built on Barton Hill was Maze St. I went there in 1908. It was horrible. When we went to school we did have to learn. No play like today. We had to learn to read and write. We always had a service. The whole school. They did mark the register and if you weren't there they did want to know why and the school board did come round to your house. The trouble was that it was such a poor neighbourhood many children never had a shoe to put on. I saw children in my class go to school with no shoes or socks – many a time.

Bertha Milton ; We used to call them the ragged boys.

Rowlie Edwards : They never had a ha'penny to call their own, some of these people round Barton Hill. It was a terrible time.

Bertha Milton : Although we had a school board officer that went to find out why anybody was absent, I was often sent after the register had been called to find out why they were away and more often than not it was because they had no shoes and stockings. Although everybody was poor at that time, some were much worse than others. So many of the small houses were only two up and two down and the families all large. There was bound to be a lot of poverty. Most years a man would come and take a photo of the class all arranged in the playground. We used to love that but we must have looked a sight with pinnies, long frocks and black shoes and stockings.

The school bell rang out loud and clear, the boys taking turn because it was their playground. I was three when I started and we had slates and used chalk in standard one. Later we had pencils and pen and ink.

Rowlie Edwards : We used to use chalk then they brought out these ink-wells. First time we ever used them we were bucked to death about them. The kiddies sat down and put his hand behind and tip them up all over your desk.

Reg Harding : We had to do copy book writing, and dictation, and pronunciation. We never had any books.

Rowlie Edwards : I went to Jarvis Street School. I went to the boys' section and they also had a girls' section. It was never mixed. There were two separate playgrounds. From there when I was 11 I went up to Barton Hill Boys's School. In Merrick Street. That was also two separate schools. We were never allowed to mix. But we did on the quiet. We used to look over the wall and see the girls out to play. And of course if we did get caught we got the cane off of Mr. Joe Baker, that was our headmaster. He was a tall man, over six foot. And he could hit them. When he did cane you he did cane you.'Hold your hand out' ...... 6 times. He didn't mess about.

Our exams were different to what they are today. We didn't do all this writing, we did get someone come round. And he did pick on us. 'You say that, you say that, you say that,' If you didn't know it, it was just too bad. The headmaster used to stand there with this school inspector.

Bertha Milton : He used to frighten us to death.

Ralph Bewley : Everything was systematic in the Barton Hill School. If I wanted a drink of water, I had to stay in the queue. There was always a monitor by the tap. And if you wanted to go the toilet there was another one there. They did keep you in line. And if you stepped out of line, they reported you.

Rowlie Edwards : Do you remember when we used to go over to the Globe and put a penny in the bucket?

Ralph Bewley : After we'd got the coal in, we took the cart back, mother used to give us the penny. We went to the Globe cinema. It was no good dropping a sweet on the floor because it sloped.

We used to try and find a big button, and throw it in the bucket. Say eight of you went in. You'd say, 'There's the eight and you'd have half a dozen ...... eight foreign coins. Mind you they had the bucket full of pennies.

There was a woman there, they had her for years. She'd come along and say, 'Come on, out!'

Bertha Milton : She was tough. Boys were just as hardened then. Worse! My mother applied for me to leave school when I was 13. And I had to go up in Peter Street before a committee. The board of education. And before then I had had to write an essay. Something to do with school days. They were all sat at a big table. I stood by myself. Mother sat on a chair at the back and I answered all the questions. Now they asked me about Wales, Scotland, the capital of Germany and the capital of France. Anyhow, I answered it alright and I got let off from school although I didn't want to leave. I knew mother wanted the money.

Bill Nicholas : That was known as the labour exam.

GOING TO WORK

Flo Melhuish : I started work at the cotton factory when I was fourteen and I started in the weaving shed at first. Wages to commence with were 3/7d per week. Out of 3/7d per week I had to pay 3d for a pocket that you put round your waist ..... Anyway, I was only there for a few days, that was before Xmas. I thought I was doing well. I was told I was doing alright. So the woman in charge said she was going down the pub to have a drink, she wouldn't be very long, and would I go on with the job. So I said 'Yes to the best of my ability I will.' If you remember I'm only fourteen. So away she goes to the pub and I gets on with the machine.

When she comes back she finds this long streak down the calico. 'Oh' she said, 'what's that, how long has that been going on?' So I said, 'for some time. What's the trouble?' She said, 'That's bad work, I don't get paid for for none of that. All that's got to be taken off and re-weaved.' So I said, 'I'm awfully sorry.' I apologised to her. I said 'I thought I was doing my best.' When all's said, she got in a temper, slapped my face and left her fingermarks on my face. So I thought, well the only thing I can do now is give her one back. So I picked up the bobbin and let her have one back see. So the foreman says, 'What's going on here?' So I said, 'Well, she slapped me across the face, you can still see the marks. I got into a bit of a paddy and hit her one with this bobbin.'

So he said, 'That's enough of that then. You go to the office and get your cards. You're finished.'
I said, 'I can't tell my mother and father that I've got the sack. It wasn't actually my fault.'
He said, 'Never mind, get your cards and out you go.'
So I goes home. My dad was in the first war, so I goes and tells him the story. I said, 'Don't tell mum 'cos it's Xmas in two days time. I'll get another job somewhere, it'll be alright.'
Anyway, after Xmas I thought I'd try somewhere else. I tried one or two places, didn't get a job, so I didn't tell my mum. I came home the same time as usual, as if I came home from work so as not to upset her. There were seven of us children. So I went back to the cotton factory and I goes up into the spinning and I sees the foreman there. Alfie Clark was his name and the white jacket man was Spafford. He was one of the managers.

Alfie Clark says to me, 'I've got no jobs this morning, nothing doing.' So I goes out on the slips and I'm crying. Spafford comes down and says, 'Hello, what's the matter with you?'
So I says, 'I've been in to ask Mr. Clark if he'd give me a job and you've got no work there, and I can't go home and tell my dad. He's an invalid and we've got seven children to keep, and we could do with the money.'

So he listens to my story and he says, 'What regiment was your dad in?' I said, 'Somerset Light Infantry.'
He said, 'So was I. Alright come into the office with me and see Alfie Clark. What can you do?'
I said, 'Anything'.
So I went on sweeping. Sweeping all the alleys out, sweeping the gangway, keeping it all clean, picking up the waste.

Rowlie Edwards talked to Mrs. Calicot, a woman who had also worked in the cotton factory:

“1912 and 1913, that was when she worked there first and she worked 6.30 in the morning to 5.30 at night, Monday to Friday. Saturdays, 6.00 till 12.30. For 4/2d a week, less 2d a week stop for the doctor. She worked in the beaming room, or weaving room, and that was right up on top of the cotton factory. If you worked more than one loom you had extra pay, 9 shillings a week. You could work more if anyone was out ill.

Bertha Milton : My mother never worked in the factory. She stayed at home. But all her sisters worked in the factory and they were fine girls. ‘Down the back lane’ it was called in those days. And it would be pitch dark when they’d go. Sometimes the lamps would be lit, but sometimes they’d be out because the lamplighter had come round and outed them. But they’d always look lovely and clean. White aprons, just a shawl round the shoulders in the first days. Long hours, not much pay. Our sisters worked in what they called the weaving. They were weavers. And on occasions when they had four looms they had what they called a helper which was a very young girl. And of course she was paid a very small wage. It was a really busy place.

There was another place where they always worked in a lot of water. They were pretty grim to see. They worked hard and they seemed to be very clannish. They were always more or less together, but they really did work very hard. And they always seemed to me rather pathetic. That’s how they appeared to me as a girl. Because I remember some of the children of those parents, very rarely had shoes and stockings to wear. On Sundays you didn’t ever see them. Of course the stone floors on all those little terraced houses and just a bit of sand strewn over the stone floor. It was two rooms, two up and two down. And when there were families of seven and eight and a mother and father. You can tell it was pretty grim. The houses were very tiny, right out on to the front door. There were no gardens or lands. And yet all those people were so clannish and so close.

Flo Melhuish : We didn’t have any canteen there to eat our food. You’d sit down in the alleyways. There was nowhere to wash your hands or anything like that. I stayed there for four or five years amongst the cotton workers. I started about 1918 just after the war. Now all the women there worked very hard. We all knew what we had to do and we knew that if we didn’t do it out we’d go. There’d be no job for you so you just had to put up with one or two things.

Hilda Edwards : I remember every now and then they used to sell the calico at two pence a yard. And I can remember seeing them coming out of the factory lunch times and going to the little shops. Pennyworth of tea, pennyworth of Nestlés milk, all put in the paper and a pennyworth of onions or whatever it might be. And I remember them coming out of the factory singing away and going off to their different streets and going away and coming back after dinner. They would go to Mrs. Young’s shop for hot water at two pence a week, supply their own tea and sugar and she did supply the hot water.

Bertha Milton : They used to sing their heads off. Come out singing. Like we go home and have tea now, they used to come home and have a quart. Have a pint. It was noted round here. The pubs were open all day then. They didn't only buy beer, they could buy a loaf of bread or a bit of sugar.

Workers leaving cotton factory

Rowlie Edwards : I can always remember them coming out with their straw hats on and their shawls. And you could hear them going down the street with their clogs on, morning after morning. You didn't want an alarm clock. They did go past your house and you did hear them singing, shouting, calling one another, 'Alice, come on Alice, it's time to get up.'

Flo Melhuish : Then you heard the stories of the different women coming into work ..... The struggles and all like that.

Rowlie Edwards : If anyone died, they never had a collection like they do today. One would stand out by the gate, with her calico apron held out for whatever they could get given. It was all given to the relatives of the one that died.

Here's what happened when they put in the stone for the church. Charles Pinney gave £300, the Cotton Factory gave £1000. And the Church Commissioners gave £500. So the Cotton Factory gave more to have the church built than what the Church Commissioners did.

Edna Howard : They probably had more ....

Ralph Bewley : I really don't know a great lot about the wagon works. because I only worked there six months. But I can remember that I left school on a Friday night and when I got home father said, "You've got to start work on Monday as a striker at the Bristol wagon works." Of course I went. It was very hard work, and it was dirty work, but I enjoyed it. I suppose we had about forty to sixty blacksmiths and you can imagine the din. Coming from school to a place where there was all fires right the way down. It seemed like the great big building was on fire. To me it was a very, very hard job.

And when we did finish our iron work, I used to grind it on the grindstone, get it cleaned up, then with father we did go up and fix all the iron work on the traps and milkfloats. When those floats were taken away from that shop, father would say, 'Go on, son, go and see them in the paint shop,' and it was glorious. All colours of the rainbow, rows and rows of them. I can remember father doing one of Banhams, the people that done animal shows on the downs. It was a beautiful thing. A caravan and it shone like glass. I was privileged to go and have a look at it.

Six months after I was apprenticed to another job, but as far as I can remember wages were between six and seven shillings a week. I was born in 1905 and you put fourteen years on top of that. It was 1918/1919. I worked from six in the morning to six at night. And till one o'clock Saturdays.

Bertha Milton : At one o'clock it was just like a regiment of soldiers coming up that lane.

Ralph Bewley : There were two entrances, one in Easton Road and one in Berkley Street. To me it was literally hundreds of people that worked there. The timekeeper, what a job he had !

The tradesmen were paid better than the ordinary labourers naturally, because they had to learn the trade. They lived in better houses. Mr. Coles over Ducie Road built all those houses, which are still standing, Lancaster Street, Stuart Street and all them round there. They were a different class of house.

The cotton factory didn't pay good wages. It was very poor, but the trades unions were gradually getting better and bigger. The blacksmiths and your engineers lived in better and bigger houses. Then you get your wheelwrights, carpenters and high class painters. They were coach painters. The body coach builder is a higher class again than the ordinary carpenter, who only does the rough work. Everything had to be made by hand. Every bit of wood in the milk float and the railway carriage. Nothing made by machine. All those men had labourers helping them.

All the carpenters, say, would get together and say, "We might as well form a union and fight and get better wages." That's how it all started.

Bertha Milton : My brother was the boilermaker trade union secretary of the boilermakers and platelayers from Lysaghts. There was a time when work began to get slack and people were put off and men were out of work. Now my brother holding that position, he was out of work. And he used to try and get men work at other places. Nobody would listen to him because he was a trade unionist. And nobody would give him a job. That's why he went to Australia.

Reg Harding : The rise of Trade Unionism and the various Guilds at this time was slow but very remorseless. Contrary to the ruthlessness of the employers who did all they could to stamp it out at birth.

Sid Hobbs : I was on the Bristol Trades and Labour Council for years. I was put there as a delegate for the union. I and Tilly Parker, the secretary, used to go round the towns such as Bridgwater, Swindon to try and get people to join the trade union movement. Of course, you hear people say that they won't join on principle. Some claim it's not christian like. But I claim, without the trade union movement you'd have little boys on the shoulders of their fathers, going down the pits at five years of age.

Rowlie Edwards : I left school at 14. My first job was working for a Mr. Bulley at Queen Anne Road, Oil and Hardware Stores. I used to go round areas all over Bristol with horse and cart selling paraffin, soap and all sorts of washing material. My first week's wages amounted to 3/-. I worked from 8.30 a.m. to 5.15 p.m. for this.

I worked at BAC for 14 years, making planes, then I was on press, making parts for planes. Then I worked on what they called the dipping. That was softening the metal that they did use in the presses, for pressing out shapes. I think the temperature was about 360 degrees. And there was salt. You did put this salt in, then you had to watch yourself or else you would get burnt. I got burnt several times. You'd put this in and leave it in about twenty minutes, and then pull it out. You used to have long iron hooks. There were two of us, one each side. We would pull it out – great long sheets. 8 foot by 4. And of course they were red hot and you had to throw them straight across into a tankful of water. They'd stay in there for about ten minutes till they were cool; then they could use them and press anything out with them. That was a nice job, I enjoyed that job, but the trouble was, it was rather risky because you'd keep getting burnt.

Bertha Milton : I was fourteen when I started in Fry's. You had to go through a thorough examination by a doctor and they wanted to know if you went to church or chapel or if you were good or no. So I had to have a tooth out and I didn't like that very much. I had to have the tooth out or else I wouldn't have gone into Fry's. I wanted to be one of their 'Angels.' If you were a 'Fry's Angel' in them days you were somebody. At

Packers, the other chocolate place here they were called 'Packers' Devils'.

The first time I ever worked in Fry's was in the weight room. Then our room had to be closed down so I had to go into a room and learn the way to cover chocolate. And I'm telling you, that was queer. For three days I had someone to teach me. And at the end of that time I had to go on piece work. It was to cover little creams which were called tens. We used to have to cover 120 for three farthings. A couple of weeks after they put it up to a penny. I didn't like it and I didn't get on very well and I really wanted to leave. But of course you couldn't leave. You had to work where you were sent, there was mother at home waiting for the money. But in those days, during the hot weather, if the work turned you didn't get any money and you were sent home. In the summer I was at home more often than I was at work. I didn't mind that a bit because I'd rather do housework. Finally I got on to chocolate creams, which are still made to this day, but today it's all done by machinery. We daren't talk, and we daren't laugh. If we laughed or if we talked we had to leave off. She'd tell you, "Leave off and sit." We had to sit on our stools and wait half an hour. And then we'd start work again. I took home one week 2/10d.

Every day we had a service. We had a hymn, then a prayer, then another hymn, then the doxology, they say. We had a choir. Of course, Fry's were Quakers.

They used to bring the boss up in a lift. He used to look a real sight. With a frock tail coat and a pair of boots on that were never done up. But I must say, when he died he left us all a bit of money, so I was alright then. If you worked there five years you had £5, and for every year over that number you had an extra pound. So I had £5 and I thought it was lovely. I was very happy in Fry's, but I was glad to leave. But I still went back there after I was married. I'm talking about before the first world war. It was drudgery really, and the pay, it was dreadful.

HARD TIMES

Sid Hobbs : We had a strike in 1916 when the war was on, and we were out about 18 weeks. There was the guardians, but there was no such thing as getting help. I had a wife and two kids and I had to live off 18/- a week. In that strike we lost two chaps, died, in the cold. It was February.

Ralph Bewley : I went right through Sunday School and I got to be a teacher. The wife and all. That's where I met the wife. I got married then after three years. I was unemployed. I had to go up Peter

Street. But previous to that, Mr. Featherstone presented my friend with the Bible and me with 'The Prodigal Son'. When I was unemployed he was one of the men on that committee.

Now I had one little boy. My wife said, when I had the sack, that she wasn't going to go on drawing unemployment for her. She was going to go into business and I had a few shares, and we bought a little business. Still owing money, but I still had to go up in front of this bench. I had two shillings a week for my boy, but he cut that out, in fact he said, "You'll have to come back later on, your wife will have to keep you."
And I said to this bloke, "Can you remember Hebron Chapel?".
He said "Yes."
And I said, "I was the boy you presented with the book. And you call that Christianity. Next time I'll stuff it down your throat."

Reg Harding : The whole family, the four boys and myself had to call up by the Board of Guardians. I wasn't married, therefore I was exempted. My three brothers had half a crown levied on them, and they had to pay it, no question about it. One of my brothers said he wouldn't pay it on certain grounds, and he told me the other Sunday that he never did. That was when the pension was 5/- a week. Then it went up to the Lloyd George pension, which was 10/- a week. That weren't sufficient so they levied the charge on the other members of the family that were working.

Ralph Bewley : You were humilated. Terrible. They didn't care what they said to you.

Bertha Milton : But Mr. Bewley, let's face it. Everybody helped one another.

Ralph Bewley : If it wasn't for your own kind I think there would have been big riots here.

Bertha Milton : My mother was left a widow, so she made an appointment through the Church, to go before the Board of Guardians. So she goes. My sister was at work then in Fry's, she was 12 years older than me, and my brother did work in a shop after school hours. Anyway, she goes before them and they said, "Well they'll think about it." And would she go outside. Now she goes outside while they all conflab. So they said they'd give her a shilling a week and a loaf of bread. And do you know they also told her that her daughter had bought a bangle at Lawrence Hill. And that was Mr. Lovelace. He was on the board of Guardians. And my mother said, "Yes and she bought it out of her own money." And after the third week after we had the bread, mother told them that they could keep it.

Rowlie Edwards : He was a devil.

Bertha Milton : My mother did go on about him, what she put up. Yet he did so well out of the pawnshop, he made his money out of that. And when he made enough money he opened a new shop.

Rowlie Edwards : You didn't know what to call him. Suppose you were ill and you couldn't get there, they'd stop it, whether you were ill or working. I went before the Board of Guardians myself, and I saw Lovelace. My father was out of work. And I was working. He looked at me, he said, "You're working aren't you?"
I said, "Yes."
He said, "Your father's out of work."
I said, "Yes." I said, "As a matter of fact he's just come out of the army. He came out and he couldn't get a job." He'd done about 27 years.
So he looks at me and says, "Well" he said, "I think I can tell you" he said "that you've got to pay." Just like that.
I said, "What do you mean I've got to pay?"
He said, "You've got to pay to keep your father."
I said, "How much have I got to pay?"
He said, "Half a crown a week."
And I had to take it up to St. Peter's Hospital, every week, that half a crown, and if I missed, Lovelace would be down our house a want to know why I hadn't been up there to pay.

Bertha Milton : They used to pawn their wedding rings. They had to get the food to last the week.

Rowlie Edwards : I can remember Swashies when they used to have a sale every now and again of the stuff that wasn't claimed, after it was there 3 months. You could buy a lot of stuff; sheets, pillowcases, suits, jewelry. If it wasn't claimed within three months it was sold.

Bertha Milton : I can remember when I was 14, going to work, and I can remember seeing women standing outside that shop, waiting for that shop to be open with a bundle under their arms. Many times of a Monday morning.

Rowlie Edwards : If you did have half a crown for a suit, you may have to pay about three pence, on top, to get it out. When you took a suit in they'd say "Half a crown." Well you wouldn't get half a crown, you'd get two and thrupence. You paid twice. You paid for putting it in and paid for taking it out. If you had a gold watch and say they offered you 30/-, if you never had that out during those twelve months, you couldn't get it out again.

Reg Harding : Shepards wasn't Barton Hill really. They ran a clothing club. People were clothed there by joining the club. 1/- a week. They used to have clothing cheques.

Bertha Milton : They used to have a 'duffer', and when he was about all the doors was closed.

Rowlie Edwards : Nobody was ever home when he did come. He couldn't get any money out of the people. As soon as they knew he was in the street the front doors was closed and they wouldn't answer the door. They knew he was there. That's why he was always called the 'duffer'.

Bertha Milton : My grandmother Summers came to live in Hayward Road, after my father died. She used to wear a little black apron, a silk apron. But underneath this little black apron, it was all embroidered, she had a thing that did tie round her waist that had two pockets. She let out money and she used to let out ten shillings. But they didn't have 10/- they only had eight. If they borrowed a pound they only had 18/-. So that's why I knew we had a little bit better than some of the others. It was nothing to do with my mother, it was my grandmother, my mother's mother, and she lived to be nearly 90. They were only too glad to lend money and borrow money.

You never had a doctor unless you paid him. We never had a doctor. If you were ill mother rubbed your chest or put something in your ear. I can never remember a doctor coming to our house.

Ralph Bewley : You used to go down the herbalist, down Stapleton Road.

Sid Stephens : I lived in Salisbury Street – it was a street of good neighbours. I well remember one lady "Grannie Hedges", she was the street 'doctor'. Any young mother who had illness, especially with children, she could tell what was wrong and could give advice free. A doctor's fee was 3/- if called to see him and if he had to call it was a charge of 6/-, a lot of money in those days.

Elsie Bolister : Our doctor used to charge 1/6d.

Bertha Milton : None of us went to a doctor and always waited until a bad tooth was loose, then someone would put a piece of cotton round it and pull it out. We'd have a good cry and it was soon forgotten.

Reg Harding : My mother was of the Victorian era. She insured her children at birth for a premium penny policy which she paid for and handed over to us when we reached the age of 21. She also put me in the Druids' Society at birth for a small sum, which ensured that the 3/- charged by the doctor for medicine was refunded on production of a receipt. I was initiated at the age of 16 and the ceremony took place at the Bush Hotel, Totterdown. It was a little frightening when the blindfold was taken from my eyes and the lodge revealed itself with members in full regalia and beards.

Bill Nicholas : You had to belong to a friendly society to get a card, in order to put a stamp on. Like the Druids or the Buffaloes or the Foresters.

Bertha Milton : In the first days of the University Settlement when a Barton Hill woman was confined and she was very poor and she came home, they would have her here, and have her here for a fortnight.

When a girl fell by the wayside she was turned out, she wasn't kept. But generally an aunt would take her in. Anyone would take them in as long as they weren't at home with their own parents. It was a terrible shame, and the talk of the place.

Hilda Nicholas : And in most firms in those days it was instant dismissal.

Bill Nicholas : They used to strap themselves up so that nobody would know.

A SHOUT OF LAUGHTER

Reg Harding : A colleague of mine who worked for Pickfords roamed the country with huge indivisible loads that the railways couldn't handle. His parents, one from Lancashire, the other from Yorkshire, were entertainers, which made him, he said, neither red nor white. He was a strong trade unionist with a golden tenor voice and was a born comedian. When the first coloured troops came to Bristol from America, they were billeted at the Drill Hall, Old Market, and frequented a pub next to the Barley Fields. I am referring of course to the Second World War. Hearing his voice I entered the bar and there he was. The troops were already in fits of laughter at his antics. He gave a classic portrayal of Hitler, worthy of a Palladium audience. His moustache was obtained by putting on soot from the open fire place. Then they pulled his leg about fighting and he gave a shadow boxing display, of Tommy Farr fighting Joe Louis and pulling their leg by saying that Farr would have won if he fought in England. This brought a shout of laughter all round and more beer. A few minutes later, a huge fellow, at least 23 stone, and athletic with it, left the bar parlour to get access to the Gents. With a huge grin on his face he said, "You know this guy Farr, he gave me a heck of a fight way back." Tommy Musgrave's face dropped for he said he was the great Joe Louis himself, and he had been sent to Bristol as a PT instructor to boost the morale of the coloured troops.

Hilda Edwards : I remember my mother taking me to see Lucy Moore.

Rowlie Edwards : She was a singer. She was 23 stone.

Hilda Edwards : I can see her now, like a big square box.

Rowlie Edwards : We used to get tickets to the Theatre Royal. You used to be able to get in for 2d with these tickets. We used to get them in a shop. We used to buy a pennyworth of sweets and on the shop counter was these tickets. And we used to take about half a dozen, when he wasn't looking.

Reg Harding : Charlie Chaplin actually appeared in the Empire as a boy in a talent spotting competition. And I saw Houdini escape from a tank, upside down.

Bill Nicholas : Mr. Day owned the Empire. He was a great supporter of the Labour Party, Harry Day. And as a result of that all the great political rallies were always held in the Empire. In those days if you were going down the Empire you were really going somewhere.

Bertha Milton : I saw Jack Johnson. I don't know whether anyone's heard of him. He was appearing at the Empire and my brothers wanted to go. I only went and watched him come out. I've never been so fascinated because he was a huge man. And of course he was black. I remember seeing him come out of the stage door.

Rowlie Edwards : Do you remember the masked man that used to fight down the Drill Hall?

Ralph Bewley : On my father's side is weight lifters. His older brothers, uncles. A couple of them came down and challenged someone on the Empire stage.

....

Bertha Milton : Women wouldn't go in pubs. You didn't. You went in the outdoor beerhouse.

Ralph Bewley : They had what you call a party of drinkers; they had a bet at our place, that this man wouldn't be sober, to start one side of Old Market Street, go up to the Park gates and come down the other side. He was a strong drinker. They had to bring him back.

Bertha Milton : Many a time you'd find a drunken man along Barton Hill. Laid out.

Rowlie Edwards : I was talking to a man who is 92 and he could remember all the old pubs all up Church Road, right up to Kingswood. There were 68.

Bertha Milton : On one occasion, I'd fallen out with Will. I didn't go with him. It was holiday time. I heard about if after when I'd made it up with him. I could only have been about 17. They borrowed this horse and trap, a two-wheeled trap. Two would sit at the front and two would sit at the back. They were going to Weston. The man at Russets told them, he said, "Well, now, you'll have to watch them mind ... " I don't know what he actually said, but he gave them some powders and he said if he don't go very well, give him a powder. Anyhow, they got to the Roddy. Even in later years you always had to get out and walk down and walk back because the hill was pretty steep. However, they get on this thing and they go, but when they get to the Roddy, they got off to get some lemonade from 'The Star'. Then the nag went quiet and wouldn't go so they gave it a powder. They were supposed to give him one powder on his way, and one on his way back, and I suppose one in between. Anyhow, they gave him all of them. Well he went down over the Roddy, and he dropped dead.

Rowlie Edwards : They used to have competitions with the cage birds. Then they used to have the pigeon fanciers: racing pigeons, two milers, tipplers and tumblers.

Bertha Milton : There was the rat catcher. He used to chop their heads off. The heads used to be put in brown paper, and they'd be hung up on the wall.

Bill Nicholas : Hopper Chinock lived in Phoenix Street. And he used to go down to Coalses the meat place down on the Feeder and he was an expert with rats. And he caught them by hand and he used to put them in a bag. On Sunday mornings on Marsh Lane bridge, the men all round used to take their whippets round and there was a road there. It's now blocked off by Lysaghts. He used to tie a string on the rats leg and he used to sell them to the chaps with the whippets. And he'd pull them out of the bag and take the string off, let the rat run down the road, and they'd hold the whippet, and the whippet had to go and catch the rat. He used to let rats run round his shirt. All sorts of things with rats.

Bertha Milton : Then he became religious and caused a revival on Barton Hill. In Morley Street.

Bill Nicholas : But he was a character. And I'll tell you another character – Joby Kirby. He was a tramp but he only tramped round Barton Hill. And the kids were absolutely scared stiff of him. Then there was Billy Balloo, he was what they called a mental defective. And there was the chap who used to wear the top hat with all the fly papers around it. Then there was the chap who used to walk round with a tin and the things he sold. The name I can remember was 'muggets'. But they were sweetbreads.

In the general strike the Welsh miners came up from Wales in groups and they had marvellous choirs and they used to sing in every street.

Ralph Bewley : All the Welshmen would come over on Saturday night, and did stay the whole day and went right through Castle Street. Because we had a lot of dance halls and all. Then they used to catch

Campbell's boat back over. There was always fighting. Then the fellows used to call a truce, say Bedminster, Barton Hill, St. Philips. When we did go up there on Saturdays we didn't fight ourselves, we fought the Welsh.

Reg Harding : They were always beautifully dressed ... always brown boots. They were mainly miners and iron workers. I know we used to go to Lawrence Hill station. When we know this train was coming in, we'd watch them. There used to be crowds and crowds. They all went one way. To Castle Street.

Ralph Bewley : West Street, Clarence Road, Old Market, Castle Street, Peter Street, Clare Street, Vine Street. There was all carts selling things – hand carts. Nothing else was allowed there Saturday night. There were literally thousands walking backwards and forwards. It was packed, all the shops open. It was marvellous. You could walk safely all the all the way through. That used to be the favourite walk when you first got married.

Bertha Milton : In Old Market they had what they called 'the Star'. You'd go in there and have a shilling dinner. You couldn't eat it all.

Rowlie Edwards : If you went upstairs you had to pay sixpence extra. We would go to the Centre, up Park Street, down by Unity Street, Wine Street, walk back down by the Infirmary. Back up to Castle Street.

Bertha Milton : We used to call it going out to pick up. "Here, did you go down last night, pick up a man?" That used to be the thing. Mind the Welsh boys were very good for buying anything.

HAVING A BATH

Bill Nicholas : Barton Hill School was noted for their swimming team, and rugby. But their swimming team really knocked the spots off anybody in Bristol. Their swimming master was a chap named Harris. You just had to swim if you were in his class. A family returned from Australia. There were two boys and their name I believe was Houselander. It's just coming to my mind. Because they were at Barton Hill School, and Harris was there, he quickly discovered that they had brought a new swimming stroke, which was called then the Australian crawl. And these Houselanders and Harris, developed it with the Barton Hill swimming team, and they knocked spots off everybody. And if you graduated from Barton Hill swimming team to Barton Hill swimming club polo team, you were really somebody. I remember a chap who was about 6ft.6ins. And his name was Joy, Bert Joy. He was the centre forward. They throw the ball into the pool and the centre forward would swim from the end of the pool to get the ball first, and flick it back, and Joy was the one who picked up the Australian crawl from the Houselanders.

Bertha Milton : Do you remember anyone else in that team? My brother was in it, Arthur Milton. He won many prizes.

Bill Nicholas : In the winter they used to put boards over the swimming baths at Barton Hill. And they called it the Palais de Dance.

Ralph Bewley : And they had boxing there.

Bertha Milton : They had hundreds along there in the winter time at the Barton Hill Baths.

Reg Harding : I used to catch little thrupenny bits, before they went down the deep end. I don't know about South Sea islanders. We kids were down there naked as the day we were born.

Bill Nicholas : At the end of the week in Barton Hill Baths when I went to swim down there, it was blacker than those shoes. The water didn't circulate. On Saturday it was as black as the ace of spades.

Reg Harding : Sunday morning they had to clean the water.

Bertha Milton : They had to empty it and refill it.

Ralph Bewley : I don't know whether you can remember the tragedy. My oldest brother. He dived in and broke his neck, from the very top stage, and that's why you couldn't dive from it.

Bertha Milton : You could go and have a bath there as long as you took your soap and your towel. Now when I went you used to pay 2d. And the woman would come and see that you didn't have too much hot water. And she'd come and see you and get you out. She'd say, "Come on out, you've been in there long enough."

Rowlie Edwards : They used to have a little peep hole. They did open this little peep hole to see if you had finished. If you didn't finish, they used to let the water out.

Bertha Milton : She was an absolute tartar, that woman, that used to have us in and out of the bath. She didn't even give you time to wash your feet.

There was no baths in the houses. As children we were bathed in a tin bath. In front of the fire. And as one came out, another one went in. And the hot water was added from the hob which was in front of the fire, and it would be lovely and warm. My oldest sister used to bath us. And my mother took over and she used to dry us, and brush our hair. Then comb our hair with a small tooth comb, to see that we had nothing alive in our head, which of course was quite a common thing in my school days.

Bill Nicholas : All the big political meetings at election times, took place at Barton Hill Baths. Because they had these boards that they put over the top. I was obviously too young to go, but as far as I can remember, the kids were involved in elections, far more than, say, my children. On election days, for instance, there used to be big trays. Gangs of kids, girls and boys, used to go round and round, vote, vote, vote, for whoever it was.

Barton Hill Baths, Barton Hill Adult School, the University Settlement, and places like this, were really the centres of life. And for the men of course it was the various pubs.

Bertha Milton : The Adult School was a very well known place. They used to have to be there at half past eight on a Sunday morning. And of course it wasn't always religious. They'd have discussions about everyday problems, and politics.

Bill Nicholas : It was one of the main institutions on Barton Hill. The building's still there and you can see how substantial it is. It now belongs to the Shaftesbury. They had a club and everything there.

Ralph Bewley : They had Quaker meetings down there.

Bill Nicholas : At Barton Hill Adult School they had a 'First Day School' there and they taught people to read and write. Anyone who couldn't read or write, who had no schooling could go to the Adult School on a Sunday morning. As it developed, the school on a Sunday morning became a kind of debating society for anyone who was interested in politics or social affairs. Working men always went to the Adult School on a Sunday morning at half past eight and it finished at about half past ten. They discussed moral, social, religious, political, economic problems of the day.

THE AIR RAIDS

Ralph Bewley : Bristol's blitz night, that was on the Sunday night, my wife was expecting our first girl. I'd already had three boys. She told me about half past four the pains were coming. 6 o'clock I went up to the warden and asked him to excuse me that night because I thought the wife was expecting and I thought I might have to rush over to the hospital. At 6 o'clock down came my brother-in-law, and he was the head one of St. George. He said, "We've had a whisper it might be Bristol tonight." Well no sooner he'd finished, the siren went. He dashes up the street to get his wife, my wife was already up there. By the time he came down, Bristol was encircled with flares. Of course, the first thing I said to the wife, "You would choose a night like this."

Edna Howard : I knew she'd get the blame!

Ralph Bewley : All of us went down the cellar. That was the worst place we could have been in. I could see all the electric cables, they were exposed, and we were beneath the water line. If the bomb would have hit anywhere near there we would have had it. We would have been drowned. My daughter was born half past twelve in the morning. I'd seen it was serious, so as the wife and family had gone down, I'd put my clothes on for air raid warden and dashed up to the post, and said, "I'm going to run round as fast as I can because I want to get the midwife." She was an air warden the same as me. She'd come up just before me and had gone out. And it seemed everywhere I was going, this was about twelve o'clock at night, through bomb-holes, all through Richmond Street, every post I got to she'd just gone on in front. I went right round the whole of Barton Hill, and in the end when I got back home she was at home with the wife.

Bertha Milton : This very night, what you're talking about, my mother never went in a shelter, she just wouldn't go. But when we told her she dressed, she had her coat on, she had her handbag, and she had her gloves on. And we put her in the cupboard. In our cupboard we had a big breadpan, and we made a seat for her and she sat there. And she was still there after the raid, she was quite near it, because the bomb, it was a five hundred pound bomb, fell in the middle of the road, and every pane of glass in Victoria Road and Victoria Parade was broken. But nobody was killed.

Rowlie Edwards : That first Sunday night we were in church. I sat in the back and I thought there's something funny going on out here. I never heard no sirens. So I went out, and I looked up and I could see all these lights coming down. I thought, 'Isn't that pretty!' then I thought, 'That's flares!' So I ran into the church and sat by the wife. I said, "We'd better get out of here." She said, "What?" I said, "There's an air raid." The vicar's up in the pulprit preaching, Vicar Bevan. So I waved my arms. He stopped immediately. He said, "Everybody down in the crypt." And we all marched down into the crypt. And we stopped there all night.

Bertha Milton : It was very strange, wasn't it. It lulled and went quiet. Half an hour after, it all started again. And when they all came back it was absolutely frightening, In the road where I lived, where the bomb fell, it broke the mains and everything. And we were all flooded. Then it rained all night, didn't it?

Rowlie Edwards : The candle factory frightened us, down Queen Ann Road. That was it. You know what wax is like when that burns. All the way up Avonvale Road they dropped bombs, that night, they dropped one in Corbett Street, they missed Beam Street, dropped one in Mildred Street, missed the next street. Every other street.

Bertha Milton : After all this some of the neighbours took us in. But I wanted to get back in because I had something in the cupboard that wasn't mine. I was taking care of it for my son. It was a bit of money. So I went over there. "Please let me go in" ...... "Oh no, you can't go in". But the next morning when it was all quiet, I crept in there quietly.

And I stepped over it all, and opened the cupboard, and I looked on the nail, and there was the tin with the bit of money in.

Most of Barton Hill survived the bombing but after the Second World War it was decided that something had to be done about the bad housing conditions that many people in the area lived under. There was a lot of feeling against losing a neighbourhood and friends that you had grown up with and there was a particularly strong feeling against replacing the housing with high rise flats.

But many people were happy to change a crumbling house, with no facilities, for a better one and much of the opposition to the plans came from local shop keepers, landlords and homeowners. In 1953 the demolition began. Many were moved to estates on the outskirts of Bristol and most of the old houses were replaced by high rise flats.

Bertha Milton : Sunday afternoons and sometimes mornings, often you heard singing in the street, an old man or woman begging. That was quite a common thing all the years we lived on Barton Hill. Life was hard for everyone, but all the neighbours were friends and very few front doors were kept shut. Now, after all these years, I'm back where my folk are and I'm very thankful, for there's nobody better than the old Barton Hill People.